MOB

MOTORBIKES

James Nixon

FRANKLIN WATTS
LONDON • SYDNEY

 An Appleseed Editions book

First published in 2010 by Franklin Watts
338 Euston Road, London NW1 3BH

Franklin Watts Australia
Hachette Children's Books
Level 17/207 Kent St, Sydney, NSW 2000

© 2010 Appleseed Editions

Created by Appleseed Editions Ltd,
Well House, Friars Hill, Guestling,
East Sussex TN35 4ET

Planning and production by Discovery Books Limited
Designed by D.R. ink
Cover design by Blink Media
Edited by James Nixon

ISBN 978 1 4451 0029 6

Dewey Classification: 629.2'275

A CIP catalogue for this book is available from the British Library.

Photograph acknowledgements
Alamy Images: pp. 13 top (David Hancock), 17 bottom (Mark Boulton); Baal: p. 29 middle (Oliver Keller &
Tilmann Schlootz); Confederate Motorcycles: p. 28; Corbis: p. 9 bottom (Jack Fields); Getty Images: pp. 8 bottom
(Tim Boyle/Newsmakers), 18 (Bryn Lennon), 27 bottom (Jeff Kowalsky/AFP); Harley-Davidson: p. 9 top; Honda
News: pp. 5 top, 7 top, 11, 13 middle, 13 bottom, 20, 29 bottom; Kawasaki: p. 12; Monotracer.com: p. 29
top (Peraves Ltd, Switzerland/www.monotracer.com); Photolibrary: p. 7 bottom (Corbis); Shutterstock: pp. 4 (Robert
Kelsey), 6 (Ljupco Smokovski), 8 top, 14, 15 top (Bill Lawson), 15 bottom (James Steidl), 17 top, 19 (Tan Kian
Khoon), 21 top, 21 bottom (Marcel Jancovic), 22 (Margo Harrison), 23, 24 top (Andrea Leone), 24 bottom, 25
(Michael Stokes), 26 (Colin Hutchings); Suzuki: p. 5 bottom; Vertika Trykes: p. 27 top (Vertika Trykes-USA, Inc.);
Yamaha: pp. 10, 16.

Cover photos: Shutterstock: top, bottom (Stephen Mcsweeny).

Printed in China

Franklin Watts is a division of Hachette Children's Books,
www.hachette.co.uk

Contents

What is a motorbike?

Motorbikes are two-wheeled motor vehicles. They are ridden by millions of people all over the world.

There are many different types of motorbike. A bike may be designed for everyday use, for speed, or for muddy off-road racing.
All motorbikes have similar parts.

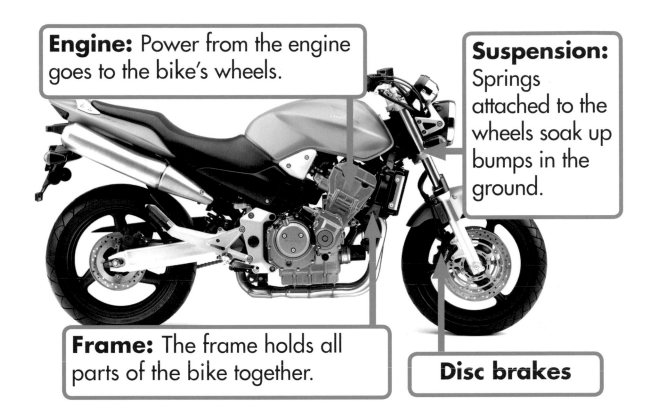

Engine: Power from the engine goes to the bike's wheels.

Suspension: Springs attached to the wheels soak up bumps in the ground.

Frame: The frame holds all parts of the bike together.

Disc brakes

Fast bike

The Suzuki Hayabusa is one the fastest road bikes in the world. This mean machine can go over 200 mph (354 kph). Its smooth shape cuts through the air at high speed.

Motorbike controls

Motorbike riders control their bikes using both hands and both feet. They use controls on the handlebars to increase speed and to control lights and indicators. They use a foot pedal to change gear.

Clutch: for changing gear

Gear change pedal

Gears

The gears change the amount of power going to the bike's wheels. If the bike is going slowly, it needs to be in a low gear. To change gear, the rider pulls in the clutch lever and moves a pedal with the left foot.

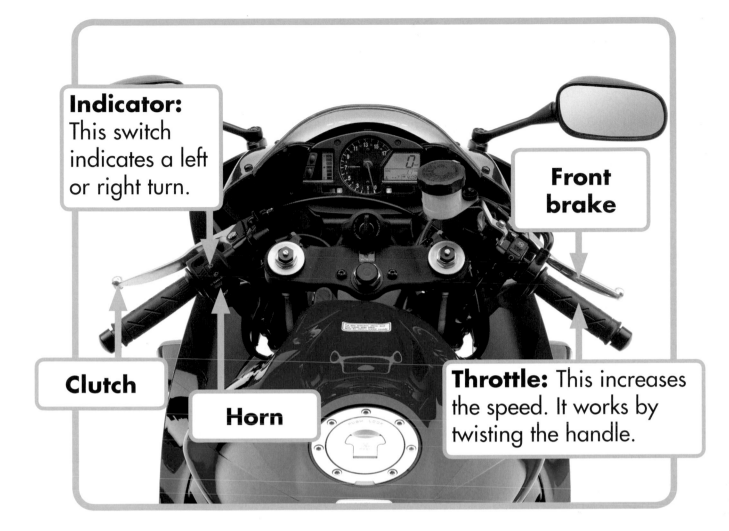

Indicator: This switch indicates a left or right turn.

Front brake

Clutch

Horn

Throttle: This increases the speed. It works by twisting the handle.

Dials in the middle of the handlebars show how fast the bike is going and how far it has travelled.

Brakes

The rider presses a brake pedal with the right foot, and pulls a brake lever with the right hand, to slow the bike down.

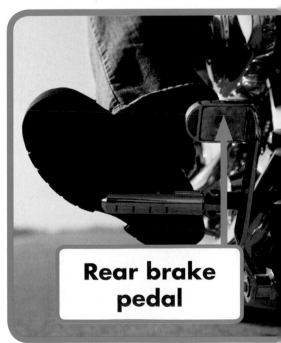

Rear brake pedal

Classic bikes

Motorbikes have been around since the early 1900s. By the 1920s they had become very popular.

Top models of bike made in the past are collected and still ridden by people today. These bikes are known as **classic motorcycles**.

Classic motorcycle

Some classics are rare and expensive. This bike made by a company called Indian was priced in a sale at £35,000.

Harley-Davidson in the USA have made motorbikes for over 100 years. Today, they still build bikes in the style of the old classic motorcycles.

Early bikes

The first motorbikes looked like ordinary bicycles with an engine bolted to the frame.

Superbikes

Superbikes are the fastest and most powerful bikes on the road. They have engines as big as a car.

The engine rests inside a lightweight frame. Their power and lightness make these bikes fast and furious.

Sidecars

A sidecar can be bolted on to a touring bike to give room for an extra person and more luggage.

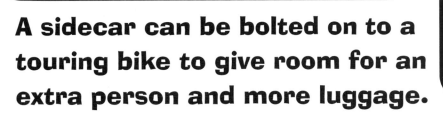

Heated hand-grips

Storage box

Touring bikes have everything you need for a long trip. The seats and hand-grips are usually heated. There is often extra equipment, such as a radio, CD player and **satellite navigation** system.

Satellite navigation

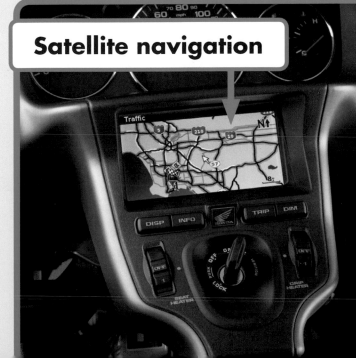

Customised bikes

Bike owners often change the look of their bikes by adding or removing parts. This is called **customising**. Customised bikes often look completely different from any other bike.

Owners of customised bikes want their machines to stand out from the crowd. They may give their bike a spectacular paint-job.

Some people add power to their bike by putting in a bigger engine. They also make the frames lighter so the bike will be super-quick.

Lightweight frame

Front forks

Choppers

Choppers are custom bikes that have had big changes. They are not easy to ride, but they look cool. The seat is low to the ground and the front forks are really long. The name comes from the fact that parts have been removed or 'chopped' out.

Scooters

Scooters are smaller, less powerful motorbikes. They use little fuel and are cheap to run.

People often drive them for short trips in cities. Scooters can be driven quickly through traffic jams. They are easy to park, too.

Parts of a scooter

Windshield

Scooters have a 'step-through frame' and floor boards for the rider's feet.

Engine: is found under the seat

Electric Bikes

When motorbikes burn fuel, fumes escape into the air. Electric bikes do not burn fuel so they are much cleaner. These bikes get their power from an on-board battery pack.

Under the seat is a recharger. This plugs into an electricity supply, and charges up the batteries when they run down.

Track bikes

Racing bikes around tracks is a fast and exciting sport. The fastest races are MotoGP races. The bikes in MotoGP reach speeds of 215 mph (350 kph).

The top superbikes on the road are raced in the Superbike World Championship. The Ducati 1098R (below) won the World Championship. One of these bikes can be bought for £25,000.

Safety gear

If a rider crashes, the only protection is his or her clothes. Riders wear a helmet and a thick leather suit. Knee pads protect their knees when they take a bend.

Knee pad

Tyres

Motorbike tyres are rounded. This helps the wheels grip the track when the bike leans into corners. In a race the rider has a choice of tyres. Smooth tyres are used when the weather is dry. If the track is wet grooved tyres are used to give better grip.

Off-road bikes

Some motorbikes are ridden off-road. They are designed to deal with rough and muddy ground.

Engine: This is high above the ground to stop it hitting any bumps.

Tyres: They are big and knobbly to grip the soft ground better.

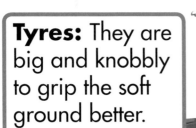

Suspension: An off-road bike's suspension is much more springy than that on a normal motorbike.

Motocross is a type of off-road motorcycle racing. Riders race around a muddy track leaping over ramps, dips and hills.

No brakes!

Speedway is another type of off-road racing. Bikes race round a small oval dirt-track, but without brakes! The drivers slide the bikes sideways round the bends.

Stunt riding

Not everyone rides motorbikes in the normal way. Stunt riders use their machines to perform jumps and tricks.

Motocross racetracks are used as arenas for stunt competitions. A group of judges look for the rider with the best jumps.

Trials bikes

In a trials competition, riders take on a dangerous obstacle course. The aim is to not touch the ground with your feet. Trials bikes are extremely light and have no seat!

Big air

Some crazy riders attempt massive jumps on their bikes. In a jumping competition called 'Big Air', riders take off a ramp and do jumps of over 20 metres!

The small and the powerful

Motorbikes come in all shapes and sizes. Tiny pocket bikes look like toys, but these are serious machines.

Pocket bikes work just like bigger bikes. Children and adults race them around tracks.

Superstar biker

Valentino Rossi from Italy is one of the best motorcycle racers of all time. The five-times winner of the MotoGP championship started his career racing pocket bikes.

Drag racers

Drag-racing bikes are the most powerful of all bikes. These machines are designed to go as fast as possible in a straight line. They can get from 0-60 mph (100 kph) in just one second!

The engine on a drag bike is so powerful it can lift the machine right off the ground. The **wheelie bar** fixed to the back stops this happening.

Wheelie bar

Big bikes, trikes and quads

Big bikes have many uses. Police forces across the world use them. They are quick, but can also carry equipment for most emergencies.

Ambulance workers use motorbikes in some cities. They can dodge heavy traffic, but still carry much of the same equipment as a four-wheeled ambulance.

Trikes are three-wheeled bikes. They are good for long trips. The extra wheel makes the bike more stable and gives the driver more room for luggage.

DodgeTomahawk

Quads are four-wheeled bikes. The Dodge Tomahawk is an amazing quad, which can travel at over 400 mph (640 kph). It needs four wheels to handle the power of the huge engine, but it can still lean into corners like a motorbike. It is not allowed on public roads.

Bikes of the future

Motorbike designs are changing all the time. So what will bikes look like in the future?

Bike makers build **concept vehicles** to show off their new ideas. They are displayed at shows first, but could end up on sale in the future.

Designers come up with some amazing new looks. This 'Renevatio' concept bike has a strange design with all its working parts on show.

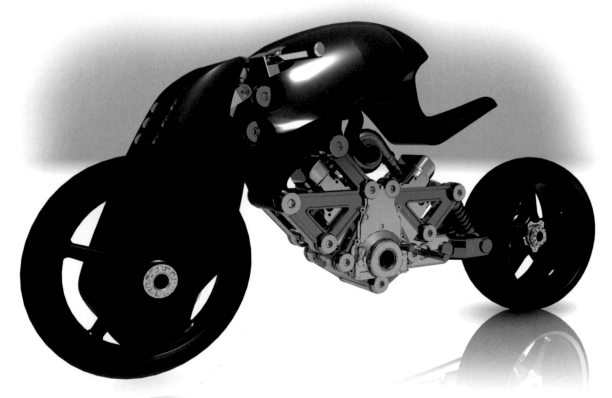

The Peraves 'Monotracer' has the thrills of a bike, but also has roof and doors like a car.

The Hyanide has **caterpillar tracks** that could pull the machine through deep mud, sand and snow.

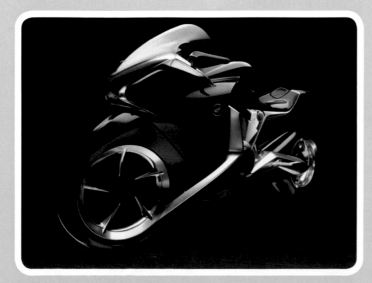

The Honda V4 (left) is a stunning concept bike. Could motorbikes look like this in a few years time?

Glossary

battery a container storing chemicals, which produces electrical power

caterpillar tracks tracks that a vehicle's wheels run on, for travel on soft and rough ground

classic motorcycles the best and most famous motorcycles of the past

concept vehicle a new design of vehicle, built for display at a motor show

cylinder a chamber inside a motorbike engine, where fuel is burnt

fuel material such as petrol or gas that is burnt in an engine to produce power

forks the supports for the front wheel of a motorbike

MotoGP a motorcycling championship for the fastest motorbikes in the world

piston part inside the cylinder of a motorbike engine, which moves up and down to provide energy to the bike's wheels

satellite navigation a system which receives signals from satellites in space to help drivers of vehicles find their way

superbikes the fastest, most powerful motorcycles

wheelie bar stabiliser attached to the back of a drag-racing bike to stop the vehicle flipping into the air

Index

Websites

http://auto.howstuffworks.com/motorcycle.htm
Find out more how motorbikes work.

www.tmxnews.co.uk/website_content/bikes
Introduction to the various off-road motorcycling competitions.

www.totalmotorcycle.com
This website is packed full of photographs, with the latest motorbike models and lots more.